PUPPETS

Lyndie Wright

Consultant: Henry Pluckrose

Photography: Chris Fairclough

FRANKLIN WATTS
London/New York/Sydney/Toronto

Copyright © 1989 Franklin Watts

Franklin Watts Inc
387 Park Avenue South
New York, NY 10016

ISBN: 0-531-10635-7
Library of Congress
Catalog Card No: 88-50373

Design: Edward Kinsey

Editor: Jenny Wood

Printed in Belgium

Contents

This book describes activities which use the following:

Adhesives: White glue (such as Elmer's), UHU and Duco cement
Beads
Brass paper-fasteners
Brushes (for glue and paint)
Cardboard or Oaktag
Cardboard boxes
Cellophane (see page 44)
Clay or plasticine
Cloth (scraps)
Coat hanger
Cold water dyes – such as Dylon
Cooking oil
Cork (from a bottle)
Cotton cloth, usually white – an old sheet would do
Dowel rods
Face paints
Feathers
Felt (scraps)
Felt-tip pens or markers (water-soluble)
Flashlight
Gloves (old)
Hole punch
India inks
Jam jars (old, for water, and for mixing white glue)
Kitchen paper
Knife (blunt)

Kraft paper or brown paper
Lights (see page 44)
Masking tape
Needles
Newspaper
Paint (poster, or tempera, paint is suitable for most surfaces; use acrylic paint for plastic)
Paper (white and colored)
Paper bags
Paper clips
Paper plates
Pen/Pencil
Pins
Plastic soda bottles (empty)
Push pins
Ruler
Sandpaper
Saucers (old, for mixing paints)
Scarf (old, silk or cotton)
Scissors
Screwdriver
Sequins
Shoe box
Staples
String
Styrofoam (balls and flat pieces)
Thin garden stakes or sticks
Thread
Trimming knife
Wire
Wood
Wooden spoons (old)
Yarn

Many years ago, when I was seven or eight years old, I made my first puppet. Forty years later I am still as fascinated as ever, as ideas and possibilities present themselves to excite me anew. The range in puppetry is so vast. From the simplest wooden-spoon puppet to complicated, thirty-stringed marionettes; from the modern abstract shapes to the traditional figures of a thousand years ago; from one-man shows to companies of a hundred – all this is puppetry.

Basically there are four main types of puppet:

1 *String puppets or marionettes*
These are jointed figures worked by strings tied to the figure and to a control (usually a wooden cross) which the puppeteer holds. A variety of materials can be used for the making of a marionette – leather, plywood, plastic wood or cloth – but string puppets are most often carved out of wood.

2 *Rod puppets*
The head and hands of a rod puppet are fixed to the ends of sticks or rods which the puppeteer holds to operate the figure. The body is of cloth, either sewn or draped. The head and hands can be made out of wood, plastic wood, cloth or papier mâché. Rod puppets usually don't have legs.

3 *Hand or glove puppets*
The head of a hand puppet can be made from wood, papier mâché or cloth, and the hands out of wood or stuffed cloth. The head and hands are attached to a sacklike cloth body and the figure is worn like a glove on the puppeteer's hand. As with rod puppets, hand puppets usually have no legs.

4 *Shadow puppets*
These are flat figures made of cardboard, plastic or specially prepared animal hide. They are worked from behind a translucent screen, with only the shadow of the figure seen by the audience.

There are various ways of putting a show together. You may want to start with a written script from a book of puppet plays, or adapt a story, fairytale or legend. You may want to write your own play based on the puppet characters you have made.

If you write your own piece or adapt a story, try out your ideas with your puppets before completing the script. You may find you want to make some changes.

Remember that puppets like to do things, not stand around making speeches! And it is only when the figure moves that it becomes a puppet and not just a toy.

Be careful to move only the puppet that is talking, so that your audience know which character is speaking.

From behind the stage or screen it is very difficult to know what your audience is going to be looking at, so have someone sitting out in front during rehearsal to direct you.

1 Here are some of the things you will need when painting the puppets and costumes in this book: India inks, cold water dyes, Tempera or powdered tempera paints, water-soluble felt-tips pens or markers, face paints and brushes.

2 Gather together the following materials for making your puppets: white glue, such as Elmers; UHU and Duco cement; masking tape, string and carpet thread.

3 For your sewing kit you will need: white cotton cloth, needles, thread, embroidery thread, string, wool, beads, sequins, felt and an old glove or two.

The simplest of all puppets are painted fingers and painted hands.

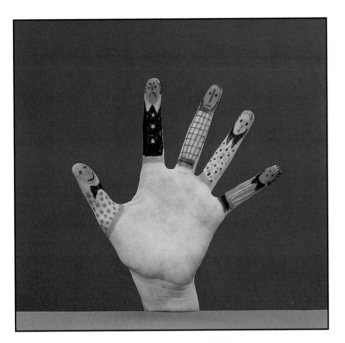

1 You can make an entire puppet company for yourself by drawing the characters on your fingers with water-based, non-toxic felt-tip pens.

2 Face paints are good for hand painting as well as face painting. You can draw either front or side views of your characters' faces. Wash your hands with soap and warm water when your show is over.

Finger puppets

You will need a piece of cloth, a
pencil, scissors, a needle and
thread, water-soluble felt-tip
pens, a paintbrush, a jar of water,
yarn or embroidery thread, and, if
required, sequins, beads and
scraps of felt.

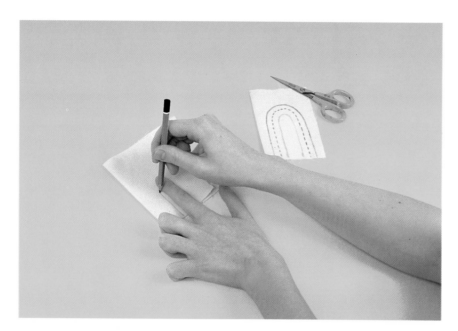

1 Fold the calico once, to make
it double thickness. Place your
finger on the folded material
and draw around it. Draw a
dotted line 1cm (½ in) away
from your first line – this will
be your stitching line. Now
draw another solid line 1cm
(½) away from your dotted line
– this will be your cutting line.

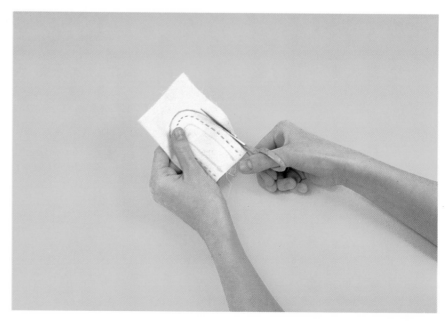

2 Cut along the outer solid line.

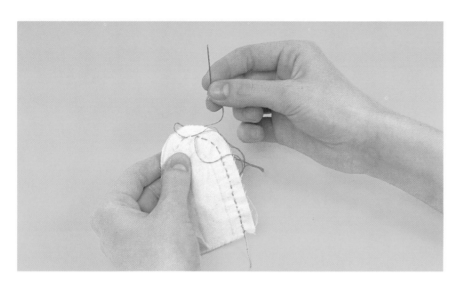

3 Thread the needle with a double thread knotted at the end. Sew along the dotted line using small stitches. Finish off the thread by sewing a few stitches on top of each other.

4 Now turn your stitched finger shape inside out.

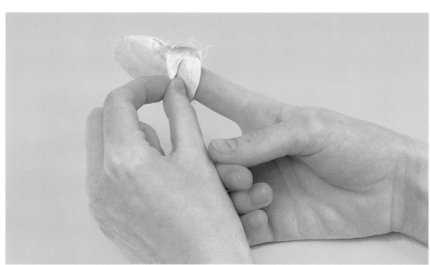

5 Color your puppet with water-soluble felt-tip pens. To make the colors flow into each other, paint over sections with a wettish brush. Experiment on a scrap of cloth before you paint your puppet to see how wet your brush needs to be. You can draw over the painted areas to strengthen the colors.

6 When your puppet is dry, add embroidery thread or yarn for hair. A felt hat may be added and decorated with sequins or small beads.

7 Your puppet or puppets are now ready for putting on a finger-puppet show.

A little finger-puppet stage can be made from an old shoe box. Simply cut away half the bottom of the box and stand the box on end to make a booth. This would look very good painted in stripes like an old Punch and Judy booth.

You will need a piece of cloth, a pencil, scissors, a needle and thread, water-soluble felt-tip pens, a paintbrush, a jar of water, and embroidery thread or yarn.

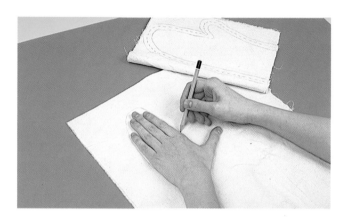

1 Fold the calico once, to make it double thickness. Place your hand on the folded material, fingers together and thumb extended, and draw round it. Draw a dotted line 1cm (½ in) away from your first line – this will be your stitching line. Now draw another solid line 1cm (½ in) away from your dotted line – this will be your cutting line.

2 Cut along the outer solid line.

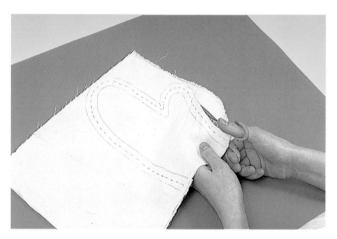

3 Thread the needle with a double thread knotted at the end. Sew along the dotted line using small stitches. Finish off the thread by sewing a few stitches on top of each other.

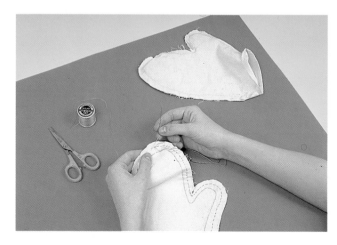

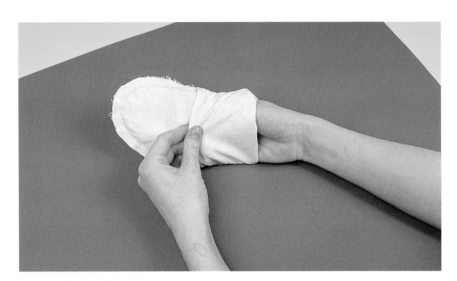

4 Turn your sewn glove inside out.

5 Color your puppet with water-soluble felt-tip pens, then wash over the color with a wet brush.

6 Sew yarn or embroidery thread on for hair, five or six strands at a time.

7 Your puppet or puppets are now complete and ready to perform.

Wooden-spoon puppets

You will need a wooden spoon, tempera or powdered tempera paints, paintbrushes, a jar of water, a saucer, white typing paper, scissors, white cloth, India inks or cold water dyes, masking tape, a feather, and embroidery thread or yarn.

1 (Left) Paint a face on the back of the wooden spoon.

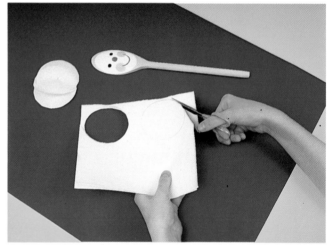

2 (Right, above) Cut out five or six circles of typing paper for the puppet's collar.

3 (Right, below) Pierce a hole in the center of each circle and thread the circles onto the spoon handle.

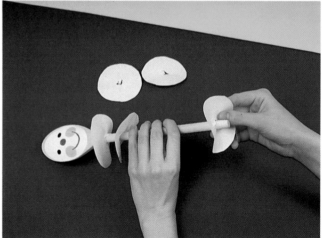

4 (Left) Cut a large circle of white cloth, about 45cm (18 in) in diameter, for your puppet's costume. Paint it with Indian inks or cold water dyes (see page 44). The puppet's neck will be in the center of the cloth.

5 Cut a small hole in the center of the cloth circle. Thread the spoon handle through this hole and fasten it to the underside of the material with masking tape.

6 Add a feather as hair, or make a thread or yarn wig instead. You may even want to make a hat to complete your wooden-spoon puppet.

An interesting puppet could be made from a wooden fork or from a dish mop. As you start to think about puppets, you will find that objects at school and in your home give you lots of ideas.

You will need a white paper plate, India inks or poster paint (tempera), paintbrushes, a jar of water, a saucer, a flat stick or ruler, masking tape, scissors, a piece of cloth painted with India inks or dyes, an old glove, pins, a needle and thread, colored paper, a blunt knife, and glue.

1 Paint a face on the paper plate using India inks or poster paints.

2 Using masking tape, fasten the flat stick or ruler to the back of the plate.

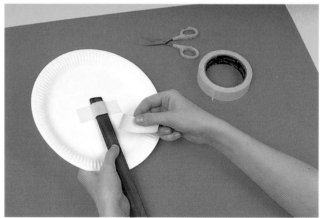

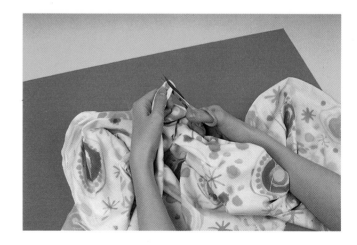

3 Cut a small hole in the center of the painted calico.

4 Slip the stick through this hole and, at the neck, fasten the underside of the material to the stick with masking tape.

5 About 14in away from the puppet's neck, make a cut in the cloth the width of your glove.

6 Place the glove into the slit, with the thumb nearest the puppet's head. Pin it; then, on the underside of the material, sew it into position.

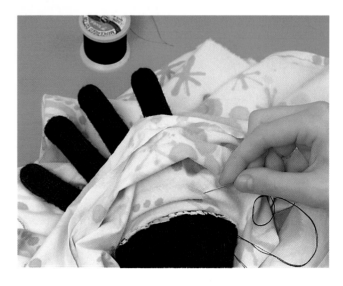

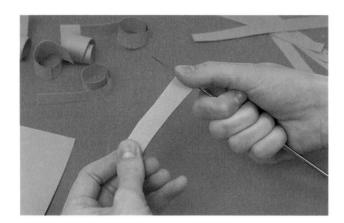

7 To make curly hair for your puppet, cut the colored paper into strips and stretch them by using the edge of a blunt knife. Hold a paper strip between your thumb and first finger and carefully pull the knife edge along the paper.

8 Glue the curls onto the paper plate. Your puppet is ready for action!

You will find the glove hand is very useful if you have to handle props. Keep your hand movements simple and clear so that the audience can follow your actions. They must be convinced that the hand belongs to the puppet and not to a person.

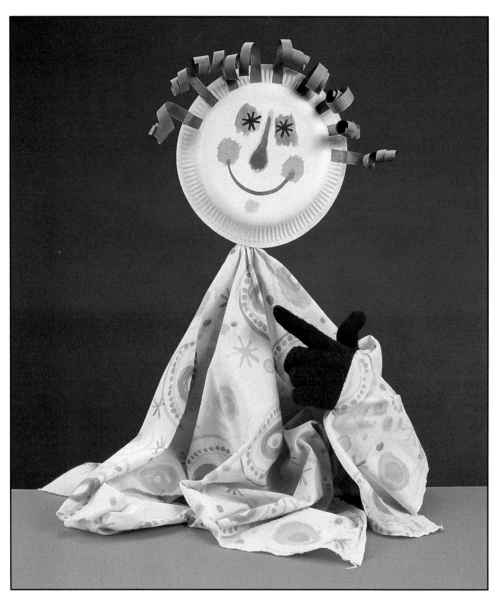

You will need newspaper, white glue, a glue brush, a dowel or stick, push pins or staples, two paper bags, masking tape, a jar of water, scissors, brown paper, poster (tempera) paint, paintbrushes, a saucer, some cloth, cold water dyes, and wool or embroidery thread.

1 Paint a sheet of newspaper with the glue. Be careful to protect the area you are working on with old newspaper, and wipe off any spilled glue before it dries.

2 Roll the newspaper loosely around the end of the dowel or stick and fix it in place with a staple or push pin.

3 Put the roll of newspaper into a double paper bag. Fill the remaining spaces in the bag with more gluey newspaper.

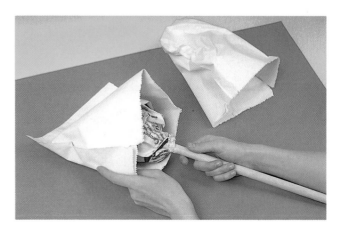

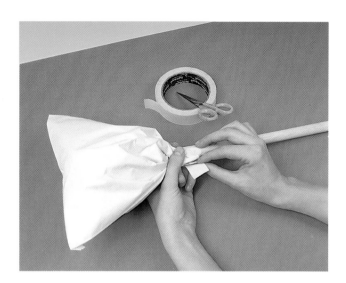

4 Tie up the neck of the bag with masking tape.

5 Flatten the pointed corners. Paint the whole bag with the glue (diluted one part glue to one part water) and leave to dry.

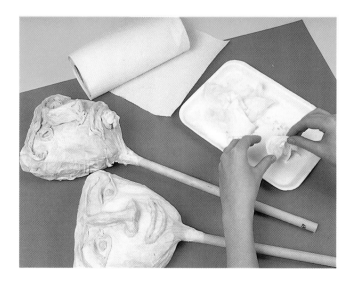

6 Build up the features of the face with kitchen paper which has been dipped into the diluted glue. Let dry overnight.

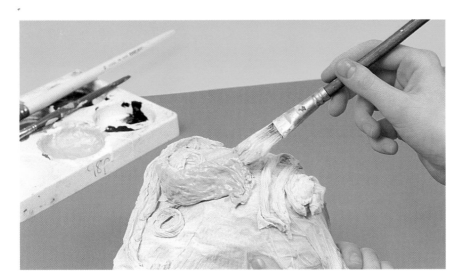

7 You will find that the features have hardened overnight and the head can now be painted with tempera paint.

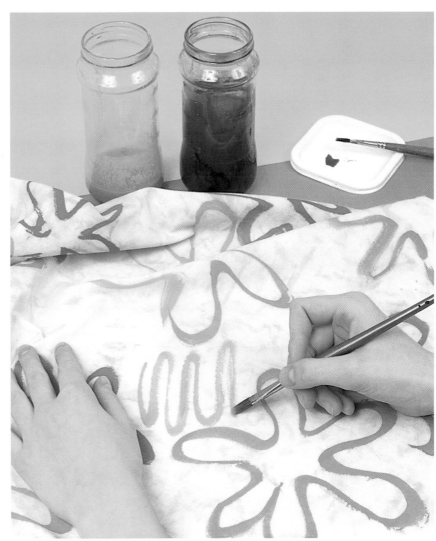

8 Make a costume for your puppet from the calico. Paint it with dye, or use a piece of colored cloth. Make a neck hole and fasten the cloth to the dowel with masking tape. Now decorate your puppet with hair and eyes.

9 Two finished paper-bag puppets.

If you need to handle props, you could use a glove hand, as with the paper-plate puppets on pages 16–18.

You will need a plastic soda bottle, scissors, masking tape, a dowel or stick, old newspaper, white glue, a jar of water, a glue brush, sandpaper, cloth, a pencil, a needle and thread, tempera paint, paintbrushes, a saucer, bits and pieces for decorating your puppet (felt, feathers, beads, yarn), fabric for your puppet's costume, Bostik, and India inks or cold water dyes.

1 Cut the top third off of the soda bottle. This top third will be the neck end of your puppet's head.

2 Cut off the bottom third. (The middle section of the bottle can be thrown away.) Cut or pull off the base of the bottle and you will find a rounded shape underneath. This bottom third will be the top of your puppet's head.

3 Make a few little cuts along the top edge of the bottom third (the edge without the domed shape) so that the two cut sections of the bottle fit easily into each other. Overlap the sections by an inch and stick them together with masking tape. You now have a very good basic head shape.

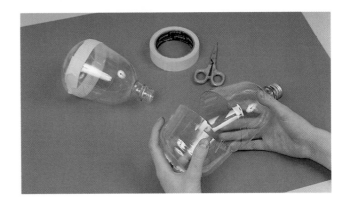

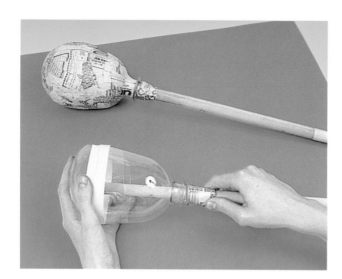

4 Push the stick up into the head. Cover the head and neck joint with three or four layers of newspaper dipped in white glue (diluted one part glue to one part water), smoothing down each layer carefully as you put it on.

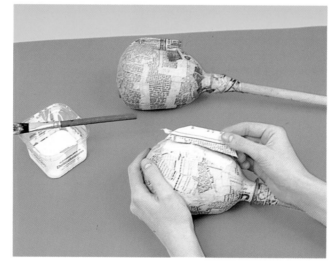

5 Make a nose by folding a strip of glued newspaper seven or eight times. Cut it to shape and glue it to the head with more bits of newspaper. Let it dry. When thoroughly dry, smooth off the head with sandpaper.

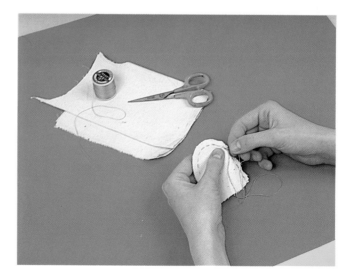

6 Make a simple little cloth hand to fit two or three of your fingers. Follow the system you used when making finger puppets (see pages 8–10).

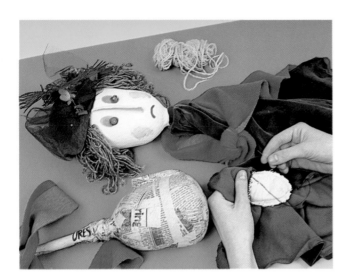

7 Paint and decorate your puppet's head. Make a costume as you did for the paper-bag puppets (see pages 19–22). Sew the hand into position as you did with the glove (see page 17). If the hand needs a touch of color to match the head, use a little diluted ink or dye.

8 Your puppet is now complete. You will find this a very expressive puppet.

You will need a Styrofoam ball, a screwdriver, a dowel, white glue, a cork, sandpaper, beads, string, scissors, a pencil, a flat piece of Styrofoam, a trimming knife, a piece of wood to use as a cutting block, masking tape, thin white cardboard, two thin garden stakes, a glue brush, tempera paint, a paintbrush, a saucer, some white cloth, and fur fabric, and yarn or string.

NB Do not use Duco cement or UHU, as these glues will dissolve the Styrofoam.

1 With the point of the screwdriver, make a hole in the Styrofoam ball large enough for the dowel to fit into. Glue the dowel into position.

2 Shape one end of the cork with sandpaper, for the puppet's nose. Cut a suitable hole in the Styrofoam ball and glue the other end of the cork into position.

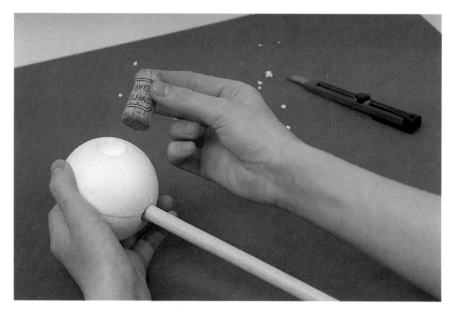

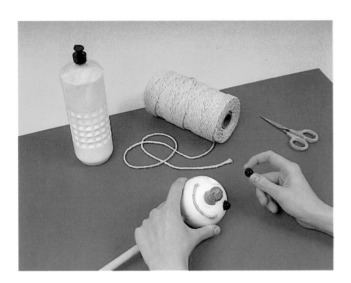

3 Cut shallow holes for the eyes and glue beads in place. Glue on a piece of string to form the mouth.

4 Draw four simple hand shapes on the ceiling tile. Lay the tile on the wooden cutting block and, using the trimming knife, cut out the hands.

5 Cut a piece of string, long enough to make both arms when tied around the dowel. Tie the middle of the string around the dowel and place each end between two hand shapes. Glue each set of two hand shapes together, and hold them in position with masking tape while they are drying.

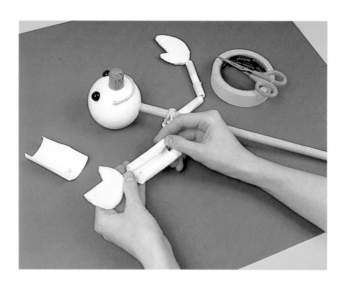

6 Make four arm tubes by rolling pieces of thin white cardboard around the pencil. Thread the cardboard pieces over the string arms and fix them in place with masking tape to form arms which that bend at the elbows and wrists.

7 Shape the hands with the trimming knife and smooth them off with sandpaper. Spike a hole into each hand and glue a thin garden stake in each. Paint the head and hands with white glue to strengthen them and let them to dry. Make sure your puppet won't stick to anything while drying.

8 When dry, paint the head and hands with poster paint. Make a costume of painted or plain cloth and cut a neck hole. Stick the cloth to the rod neck with masking tape.

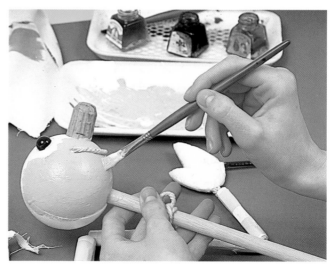

9 Decorate your puppet's head with fur fabric, yarn or string. Your rod puppet is now complete and ready for action.

To operate the rod puppet, hold the head rod in one hand and the two arm rods in the other. This may feel awkward at first but you will soon get used to it.

You will need a dowel, a bottle to use as a modeling stand, clay or plasticine, a spoon for modeling and hollowing out the puppet's head, cooking oil, white glue, a jar of water, newspaper, sandpaper, a pen, a trimming knife, thin cardboard, a glue brush, masking tape, tempera paint, a paintbrush, a saucer, bits and pieces for decorating your puppet (felt, string, beads, iron-on tape etc.), a needle and thread, and an old glove.

Cover all working surfaces before you start, as both clay and papier-mâché are messy to work with. Wear an apron or old shirt and wash off any spilled glue before it dries.

1 Stand the dowel in the bottle and model a head on it with clay or plasticine. Make the features bold and simple, since fine detail will get lost when you cover the head with paper. When you have finished the modeling, smooth the head with cooking oil to make separation easier when you come to hollow out the clay.

2 Thin some white glue (diluted one part glue to one part water). Dip postage-stamp-size bits of newspaper into the glue mix and place them on the modeled clay head, overlapping them each time and smoothing down each piece. Five or six layers of newspaper will be needed. When finished, leave the head to dry overnight in a warm place.

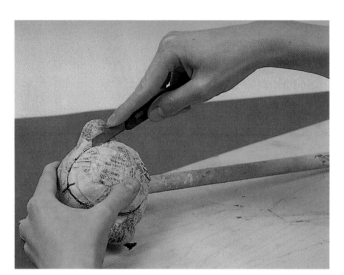

3 When the head is dry, smooth it off with sandpaper. Draw a large circle over the top and back of the head. (Put a few marks across the line to help you match up the pieces when you have to rejoin the head.) Now cut out the circle with the trimming knife. If your papier-mâché is very thick it can be quite tough, so get some help from a responsible adult.

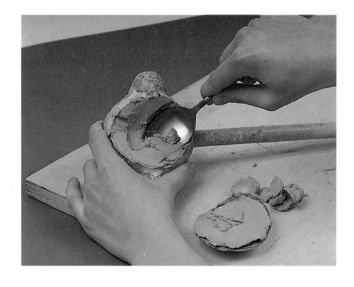

4 With the spoon, carefully remove all the clay from both halves of the head. If parts of the papier-mâché are too thin, paste more paper on the inside of the head.

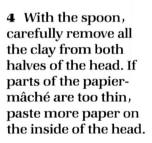

5 Remove the dowel. Match up the two halves of the head again and join them with strips of glued paper.

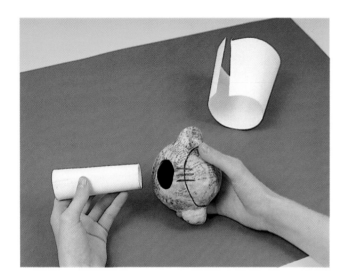

6 Roll some thin cardboard around your index and second finger to make a neck tube. Paint the overlapping cardboard with glue and hold it together with masking tape while drying. Cut a neck hole in the head to fit the neck tube. Fix it in place with more glued newspaper and let it dry thoroughly.

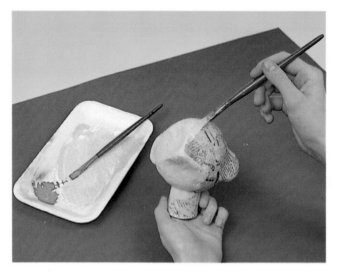

8 Smooth off the neck and head with sandpaper, and paint with poster paints (tempera).

9 Decorate the head with eyes, hair and a hat. This puppet has a cardboard hat covered with felt and his hair is sisal string painted with dye (just lay the string on newspaper and paint it). The eyes are little wooden beads cut in half. The ruff is a long strip of Vilene folded and sewn at one end, top and bottom, then tied around the neck.

10 The body is very easy to make. It is simply a glove with a few felt circles sewn onto the front.

Your first two fingers work the head; your thumb becomes one of the puppet's hands and your little finger and the next one become the puppet's second hand. These last two fingers need to move together so that the puppet doesn't appear to have too many arms. If you are making a girl puppet you can sew a skirt on to your glove just below the thumb.

This puppet has a lot of very good movements. By twisting the two neck fingers, you can make him shake his head. He can nod, bow, pick up props, jump up and down when happy, and clap his hands. He can also look very sad.

You will need a cardboard box, a pencil, scissors, Duco cement, white glue, a glue brush, tempera paints, paintbrushes, a saucer, an old scarf (silk or cotton give the best movement), masking tape, black thread (linen carpet thread) or thin string, a large needle, and a coat hanger.

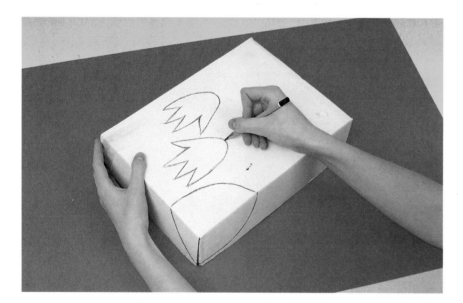

1 Draw the puppet's head on a corner of the cardboard box. The top of the head should be flat. Draw the hands on the box as well. Keep the hand shapes simple so that the fingers don't break off.

2 Cut out the face and hands and fold the fingers a little to make a more three-dimensional shape.

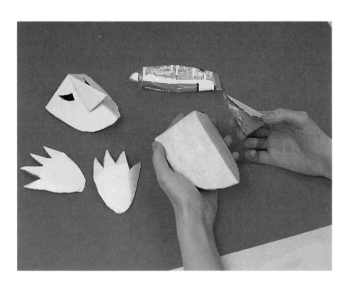

3 Cut out a cardboard nose and stick it onto the face with Duco. Draw and carefully cut out eyes. To strengthen your puppet, give the face and hands a coat of white glue. When the glue is dry, paint the puppet with white or colored paints.

4 Using masking tape, fix the head and hands to three corners of the scarf, leaving the fourth corner free to trail behind the puppet.

5 Thread the needle with the thread or string and knot the end. Bring the needle up from the palm of one of the puppet's hands and tie the thread or string at one end of the coat hanger. The length of your string should equal the distance from your elbow to 15in from the ground. Now do the string for the other hand. The two head strings go from the widest points at the top of the head to two points about 5in apart at the center of the coat hanger.

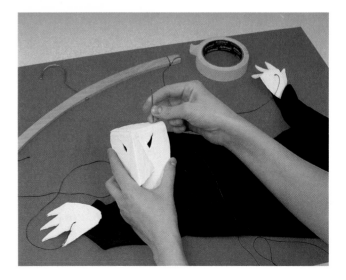

6 Your puppet is now complete and you will find it very exciting to work. You can either just hold the coat hanger and whoosh the puppet around or you can lift a hand or head string separately. The movements can be quite magical and very ghostly if you do them slowly.

You will need thin white cardboard, a hole punch, India inks, dyes or felt-tip pens, cooking oil, brass paper fasteners, masking tape, thin rods, glue, a screen, and a light.

1 Draw the various pieces of your puppet on the cardboard. Allow for the fact that where the pieces join, the cardboard will have to overlap. The joints will give you movement, so plan your puppet accordingly.

2 Carefully cut out the various pieces and punch holes for the joints.

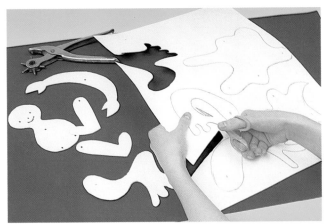

3 Paint the pieces with India inks, dyes or felt-tip pens. Keep the colors strong, and paint both sides of each piece – hold them up to a window to make sure the two sides match.

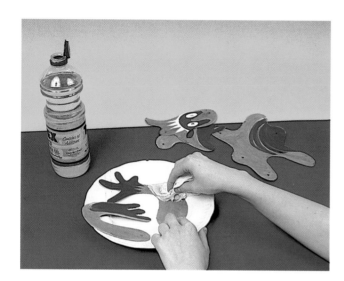

4 When the pieces are dry, rub them thoroughly on both sides with cooking oil. Keep oiling them until they become translucent, then rub off any extra oil.

5 Now join the pieces together with the brass paper fasteners. Keep all the smooth heads of the fasteners on one side. This will be the side of the puppet which is held against the screen.

6 Roll a piece of masking tape around one end of each rod. Glue one rod (masking tape end) to each of the puppet's hands. (Use UHU glue, as it will stick to the oiled cardboard.)

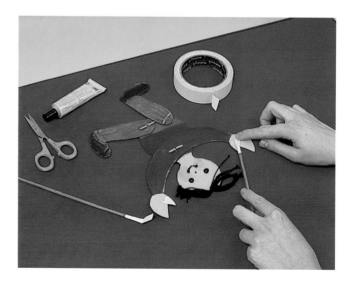

7 The puppeteer's view of the screen.

8 The audience's view.

The screen can be made of stretched sheeting, window blind fabric, architect's linen or any material that will let the shadow of the puppet show without the light element being too noticeable – this is very tiring to the audience's eyes.

A 100-watt reading lamp or projection light will be suitable. Keep the light either higher or lower than the puppeteers so that only the puppets show on the screen, not the puppeteers' shadows.

Get some help with the setting up of the light, since it needs to be very stable.

You will need two cardboard boxes of the same size (wine boxes are a good size and are strong), a pencil, scissors, tempera paint, paintbrushes, a jar of water, a saucer, masking tape, garden stakes, thin cardboard, thin wire for hooks (paper clips could be bent to shape), a flashlight, and cellophane.

1 Mark a proscenium, or stage opening, on the front of one of the boxes and cut out the opening.

2 Paint the outside of the box, as well as the inside floor and the inside back wall. The inside back wall will be your final backcloth or skycloth.

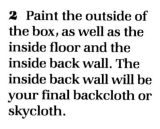
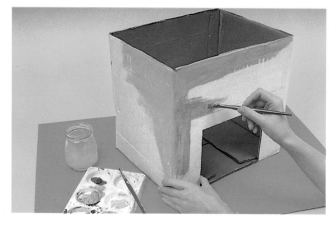

3 Draw and paint the scenery on pieces of cardboard from the second box. This scenery will slide into the first box.

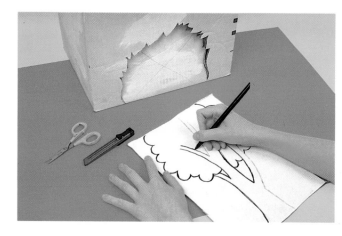

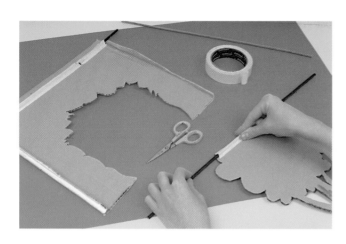

4 Using masking tape, fasten a garden stake along the top of each piece of scenery. Allow extra at either end, so that the rods stick out beyond the width of the box.

5 Put the scenery in place by resting the stakes in grooves cut in the top of the box sides.

6 Draw and paint puppets on thin card then cut them out. Paint the backs of the puppets on the reverse of the cardboard, so that the puppets can turn around.

7 Using masking tape, fix garden stakes to the puppets as you did with the shadow puppets (see pages 37–39). Now fix wire hooks to the stakes. Position the hooks so that when the puppets are hooked to the scenery, they will be able to stand without being held. This is especially useful if you are doing a one-man show.

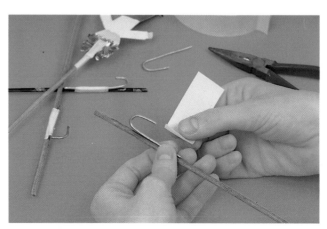

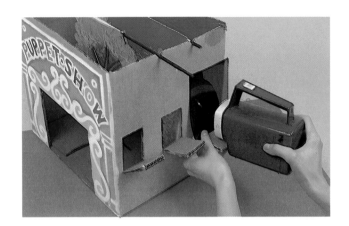

8 Cut lighting slots in one side of the box so you can use a flashlight to spotlight the puppets. Make exciting colour changes in your lighting by sticking colored cellophane or theatrical gels over the slots.

9 A finished toy theater in action.

1 For this stage you need two chairs and three pieces of wood. Tie two upright pieces to the chairs, top and bottom. Now tie the third piece across to form a "playboard", where the puppets perform. Hang cloth from the playboard to hide your puppeteers. Scenery can be drawn, cut out and pinned to the upright pieces of wood, thus leaving an acting area in the center for your puppets.

   The same stage could be used for string puppets. You would then hold the puppets out over the playboard and work them on the floor. A reading lamp or two could be very useful to light the puppets.

2 For this "Doorway Shadow Theater," you need to fasten an old sheet across a door. You may need an adult's help. Choose a doorway that won't be needed while you rehearse and perform. Now fasten another, thicker cloth across the bottom of the door, so the shadow of your head is just out of view when you kneel.

   Shine a light onto the sheet. A 100-watt light bulb is usually strong enough for a shadow screen. Mount it higher than your head so that your own shadow isn't thrown on the screen.

   Try some special effects with your light. You will find that by moving toward the light, some small sections of your puppets can be blown up to fill the screen without losing any of the detail or blurring their form.

   Your audience will sit on the other side of the screen to watch the show.

Stationery stores and/or art-supply stores and stores such as Woolworths will carry most of the items listed in this book. Specialist materials (or materials in large quantities) can be purchased through school supplier's catalogs. One supplier is Hammett, Box 545 Hammett Place, Braintree, MA 02184. Also, check the Yellow Pages in the telephone book under Artist's Materials and under Craft Supplies.

Adhesives

Elmer's Wood glue, is excellent for papier-mâché, Styrofoam, and most surfaces that don't need instant sticking. Any excess will wash off when wet. Duco cement is clear and will stick most surfaces instantly, but do *not* use it on Styrofoam as it will dissolve the surface. UHU is the best glue for oiled shadow figures.

Dyes

Dylon Cold Water Dyes are ideal for painting cloth, but ignore the instructions printed on the container, as these refer to dyeing fabric by soaking it. Instead, mix the dye in a jar with a little cold water, and test the colour first on a small piece of cloth. Remember that the color will always dry lighter.

Felt-tip pens

Water-based felt pens are best for drawing on cloth puppets, as you can get interesting effects by spreading the colors with a wet brush. But water-based felt-tip pens are not waterproof, so you will have to keep your puppets very clean as they won't stand washing. Spirit-based felt pens are more waterproof and are the best ones to use on plastics, but you can't spread the colors.

Lighting

When lighting your puppets, a couple of reading lamps with 100-watt bulbs will probably be enough. You can use colored cellophane to change the color of your lights, but don't put it too near a hot lamp for long since it will burn. An alternative to colored cellophane is theatrical gels, a non-flammable color filter for theater lights. Consult the Yellow Pages in the telephone book under Theatrical Equipment and Supplies.

Since the beginning of history, people have used puppets to tell a story. In tombs of ancient China, India, Egypt and Greece we find remnants of early puppets. The early Greek figures are very similar to puppets used in Sicily and Belgium today. An iron rod is fixed to the head, and the arms and legs are worked by strings or rods.

As the people of the Mediterranean moved around, it is likely that they carried puppets along, introducing them to countries such as Italy. We know that the Romans had both marionettes and glove puppets. After the fall of Rome, the puppeteers joined the acrobats, jugglers and minstrels who wandered all over Europe performing in castles and market places.

The early Christian Church, too, found puppets useful. They were a way of teaching Bible stories to the many people who could not read or write.

In 16th century Italy, puppets were used in a form of comedy theater called the *Commedia dell' Arte*, about a group of clowns still known as Harlequin, Scaramouche, and Punch. These stock characters worked within a standard set of plots, but with improvised dialogue, like the Punch and Judy performers of England.

In countries such as Indonesia, China and Japan puppets have always been an important part of the culture, often having strong religious significance. In North America, too, Indian tribes used puppets in religious ceremonies long before European settlers came.

Although the United States lacked this long tradition of puppet shows, the ethnic groups that settled here brought their puppets with them, into the "melting pot." And in the 1930s, puppeteers such as Bil Baird and Burr Tillstrom (who invented *Kukla* and *Ollie*) brought puppets to American television. Later, Jim Henson came up with the *Muppets*, featured on *Sesame Street*, and now shown in fifty countries.

Today puppet shows are a source of pleasure and excitement for both adults and children all over the world.

Children's Museum of Manhattan
314 West 54th Street
New York, New York
(212) 765-5904

Brooklyn Children's Museum
145 Brooklyn Avenue
Brooklyn, New York
(718) 735-4400

Newark Children's Museum
49 Washington Street
Newark, New Jersey 07101
(201) 596-6550

Washington Children's Museum
4954 McArthur Boulevard
Washington, D.C.
(202) 337-4954

Children's Museum of Los
Angeles
310 North Main Street
Los Angeles, California
(213) 687-8800

For more information, addresses
that may be useful are:

Mrs. Allelu Kurten
General Secretary
UNIMA U.S.A.
Browning Road
Hyde Park, New York 12538

Gayle G. Schluter
Chairperson
Puppeteers of America
Five Cricklewood Path
Pasadena, California 91107
(Publishes Puppet Journal
quarterly)

The Educational Puppetry
Resource Center
294 29th Street
San Francisco, California 94131
(Publishes Puppetry in Education
News)

The National Puppetry Institute
Box U-127P
The University of Connecticut
Storrs, Connecticut 06268

The Puppet Center
32 Station Street
Brookline, Massachusetts 02146

Various puppet troupes tour
schools and libraries across the
country. They also make
appearances at local performing
arts centers, festivals, fairs and
amusement parks, as well as local
community centers. Check the
bulletin board at your library or
school for announcements, and
check your local papers for listings.

Puppets, Methods and Materials, Cedric Flower and Alan Jon Fortney, 1983, Davis Publications, Massachusetts.

Puppet Plays and Puppet-Making: The Plays, The Puppets, The Productions, (Rev. ed.), Burton Marks; Plays Inc, Boston.

Puppet-Making, Chester J. Alkema, 1971, Sterling Publishing Co., New York.

The Puppet Book: Everything You Need To Know For Putting On A Puppet Show, Helen Jill Fletcher and John Deckler, 1947, Greenberg, New York.

Marionettes: A Hobby For Everyone, Mabel Frieda and Les Beaton, Crowell, New York.

Punch and Judy: A Play For Puppets, Illus by Ed Emberley, 1965, Little, Brown and Company, Boston.

Marionettes: Easy To Make, Fun To Use, Edith F. Ackley, 1939, Illus., Lippincott/Harper Junior Books; New York.

The Master Puppeteer, Haru Wells, 1976, Illus., 192p, Crowell Junior/Harper Junior Books.

Storytelling With Puppets, Connie Champlin and Nancy Renfro, 1985, ALA.

Small Wonder: The Story of the Yale Puppeteers and the Turnabout Theatre, Forman Brown, 1980, Scarecrow.

Marionettes: How To Make and Work Them, Helen Fling, 1973, Dover.

Puppets For Beginners, Moritz Jagendorf, 1971, Plays Inc., Boston.

Folding Paper Puppets, Shari Lewis and Lillian Oppenheimer, 1964, Stein and Day.

Space Age Puppets and Masks, M.C. Green and B.R.H. Targett, 1969, Plays Inc., Boston.

Modern Puppetry, A.R. Philpott, 1966, Plays Inc., Boston.

Puppet Circus, Peter Fraser, 1971, Plays Inc., Boston.

PRINTED IN BELGIUM BY
proost
INTERNATIONAL BOOK PRODUCTION